CCSS **Genre** Realistic Fiction

**Essential Q**
How do you e
important to y

M000187434

Tell Me the
Old, Old Stories
by Marie Langley
illustrated by Amerigo Pinelli

Chapter 1
Here We Go Again......................... 2

Chapter 2
The Same but Different 6

Chapter 3
The Big Picture 11

Respond to Reading 16

PAIRED READ Family Ties 17

Focus on Literary Elements 20

Chapter 1
Here We Go Again

"Manuel?" Mama began calling as soon as she hung up the phone. "Manuel! Where are you?"

His mother appeared in the doorway. "What is it, Mama?" Manuel asked, following her into the kitchen.

Mama began searching the cupboards. "That was Grandma on the phone," she said, smiling at Manuel over her shoulder. "We're going to her house on Sunday."

"Why? What's happening?" Manuel sat down at the kitchen table. He had a sudden sinking feeling in his stomach.

"Your uncle Pablo is in town. We're having a big family party at Grandma's so we can all catch up. Won't that be great?" Mama was busy putting ingredients on the counter. "I'm going to make my special almond and orange cake to take along."

"Cool," said Manuel, but that was not what he was thinking.

Manuel watched his mother searching for her special cake recipe. While she looked, she kept talking about who would be there on Sunday.

"Antonio and Elma are definitely coming, and so are their kids. I haven't heard from Tomas, but he'll be there for sure. Oh, and I must make sure Gabriela knows!" Mama quickly wiped her hands on her apron and grabbed the phone.

Manuel listened to her telling Gabriela about Sunday—what she could bring and who would be there. Manuel's thoughts were elsewhere, though. Sure, these family get-togethers were fun. Well, they used to be, but over the last year or so, he had grown tired of them. Plus, this party on Sunday was going to mean missing out on baseball with his buddies.

"I wish I didn't have to go," thought Manuel, but he did not say anything to Mama. How could he when she was so excited about seeing all her family? He made himself return Mama's smile as she went back to checking her ingredients.

"Is it okay if I use the phone, Mama?" Manuel asked as he stood up from the table. "I need to call Vincent and tell him I won't be at baseball on Sunday."

"Sure, go right ahead," said Mama. Her mind was still on making the cake and whatever else she needed to do for the party.

Manuel took the phone and walked back to his room, dialing Vincent as he went. By the time he was in his room and closing the door behind him, Vincent had answered.

"Hey!" said Vincent. "How's it going? Are you all set for baseball on Sunday?"

"No, that's why I'm calling," said Manuel. "I can't come to baseball this week because I have to go to a big family thing at my grandma's place."

"That sounds cool," Vincent replied.

"You're joking!" Manuel scoffed. "All everyone does at these family things is tell the same old stories over and over. And then they start looking at all the old photos. I'd rather do anything else. Seriously, I'm only going because Mama would be upset if I said I didn't want to."

"Well, I think it sounds cool," said Vincent, "and maybe it'll be better than you think. Catch you later."

"Okay, see you," replied Manuel. He was slightly puzzled. Did Vincent really mean that the party sounded cool? Maybe he was just being sarcastic.

STOP AND CHECK

Why doesn't Manuel want to go to the family party?

Chapter 2
The Same but Different

"Ahh! It's so good to see you!" Grandma wrapped Manuel and Mama in hugs. She had an amazingly strong grip for such a tiny woman, Manuel thought. He hugged her with one arm and juggled Mama's cake with the other.

"It's good to see you, too, Grandma," Manuel told her.

Grandma hustled Manuel and his mother through the house. "Most of the others are here already, out in the yard," she told them. As they made their way outside, the sound of voices grew louder.

Uncle Pablo was there, and so were lots of other family members. Manuel put Mama's cake on a table that was already crowded with food. Grandma always said that making and sharing food was an expression of love in their family and that they had tons of both!

Manuel wanted to join some of his cousins, but reaching them was not going to be easy. First, Uncle Pablo draped an arm across Manuel's shoulder and told him how much he had grown. Then, Aunt Carlota planted a big kiss on his cheek and said he was looking more like his grandpa every day.

More family members arrived. Manuel felt as if he were inside a washing machine. He was being tossed around from person to person and from one hug to another. Voices and laughter flooded over and around him. Family gatherings were always like this, especially when everyone first arrived.

A while later, Grandma clapped her hands. "Time to eat!" she called. "Come and help yourselves before this table collapses under the weight of all the food!"

Soon everyone had found a place to sit. They balanced their loaded plates on their knees or on the edges of the table. The conversation and laughter died down as the focus turned to eating.

"You haven't tried any of my chicken drumsticks, Pablo," said Gabriela. "I wonder why?" There was a burst of shared laughter.

"I think you know why," Pablo replied with a chuckle. Manuel knew what would follow—the story of how Gabriela had once placed what she said was a pot of chicken stew in front of Pablo. When he lifted the lid, out flew a real live chicken!

Surely everyone there knew that story? It had come up so often at these family gatherings. Someone called out, "Come on, tell us, Pablo!" and sure enough, Pablo began retelling it.

As Manuel half listened to a story he practically knew by heart, he started thinking about what Vincent had said. Was this cool? Well, it was pretty funny, and everyone was laughing. Then Manuel realized there were things he still did not know about that story, even though he had heard this tale so many times before.

As the laughter died down, Manuel asked, "Where did the chicken come from?"

"From our neighbor Sophia," said Gabriela. "She had lots of chickens!"

"Oh, yes!" Manuel's mother exclaimed. "Papa was always threatening to eat them!" There was more laughter.

9

"So Grandpa was still alive then?" Manuel asked.

"It was soon after your grandpa had passed away," Grandma said, "but he would have enjoyed the joke." There was a murmur of agreement, and then Pablo began the story about the bag of worms and how he paid Gabriela back.

Grandma moved to sit beside Manuel. "It is good to hear you ask about your grandpa," she said. "You look so much like him. Some day soon, I will show you some photos you haven't seen before." Manuel realized he would like that.

STOP AND CHECK

Why was Manuel more interested in the old stories this time?

Chapter 3
The Big Picture

A few days after the party, Manuel called Grandma. He had not stopped thinking about the photos she had promised to show him. Manuel really wanted to see them, and he wanted Vincent to see them too. If Vincent had not made that remark about family gatherings being cool, maybe none of this would be happening.

"Is it okay if I come over, Grandma?" Manuel asked.

"Of course, Manuel, come anytime!" said Grandma.

"Can I bring my friend Vincent? You've met him before." Manuel did not have to explain any more.

"Oh, yes, I remember Vincent. He's the one with the very short hair," Grandma jumped in. "I look forward to seeing you both. Now I'll search for those old photos. *¡Hasta pronto!*"

Then Manuel called Vincent. "Do you still want to come with me to my grandma's this afternoon?" he asked. "Grandma says it's fine, and Mama will drop us off on her way to the store."

"Let me ask my mom, but I'm sure it'll be okay," replied Vincent. When he came back to the phone, he announced, "I'm on my way!"

Mama was happy to drive Manuel and Vincent to Grandma's house. "I'll pick you up in an hour or two," she said. "Tell Grandma I'll see her then."

"Sure, Mama. See you soon." Manuel and Vincent climbed out of the car, and Grandma came out onto the porch and waved as her daughter drove away.

"Come on in," Grandma called to the boys. "I have fresh orange juice and a snack waiting for you. I know how you growing boys are always hungry!"

When Manuel and Vincent could not eat or drink any more, Grandma cleared the table and brought out a suitcase. It was small and battered and looked very old. Grandma hesitated before she opened it.

"These are special pictures, Manuel," she said. "When I show them, it is like introducing your grandfather himself. It is sad that you never met, but that is how things are." Grandma sighed, but then she smiled at Manuel and Vincent as she opened the suitcase.

The next hour passed very quickly. Each photo showed Manuel's grandpa at a different stage of his life, from childhood to middle age when he passed away.

With each photo, Manuel asked questions such as "Who is this?" and "When was this one taken?" Grandma answered all his questions, seeming to savor every moment of telling the boys about Manuel's grandfather.

There was one very old photo, taken in a barren Mexican landscape. It showed a horse with feathers in its bridle. A small boy sat in the saddle, staring proudly at the camera while a man and a woman stood watching him.

Grandma held the photo and gently touched the plumes in the horse's bridle, imagining the softness. "This is the only picture of your grandpa's parents," she said. "He didn't remember what else happened that day or who the horse belonged to. He only remembered sitting there with his mama and papa watching."

Grandma packed the photos away—it was time to come back to the present. Mama arrived with groceries for Grandma, and they chatted as they put everything away. The boys waited outside on the porch.

"You didn't say much in there," Manuel said to Vincent. "Is everything okay?"

"Sure." Vincent gave Manuel a meaningful look. "I just think you're lucky to have a grandma and lots of family, and all those old photos."

"Don't you have that stuff, too?" Manuel asked him.

"I never met any of my grandparents," said Vincent. "I only have one aunt, and she lives in Canada."

"Well, you can come to our next family gathering if you want to." Manuel understood now that these occasions were special and worth sharing.

STOP AND CHECK

Why does Manuel invite Vincent to the next family gathering?

Respond to Reading

Summarize

Use important details from *Tell Me the Old, Old Stories* to summarize the story. Your graphic organizer may help.

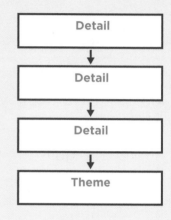

Text Evidence

1. How do you know that this story is realistic fiction? GENRE

2. What is it about family that Manuel wants to share with Vincent? How does Manuel's sharing with Vincent help communicate the story's theme? THEME

3. What does the simile on page 7, "as if he were inside a washing machine," mean?
   SIMILE AND METAPHOR

4. Write about what is important to Grandma and how she expresses this. How does this support the story's theme? WRITE ABOUT READING

Compare Texts

Read a poem about the special times a girl has with her family.

Family Ties

There are gulls flying high in the sea-blue sky.

They swoop down and spy on Grandpa and me.

But we're too busy to care—we're building
down here

A castle as grand as a castle from sand

Is ever going to be.

"Quick!" says my grandpa. "Dig fast and dig deep!

It's a ditch that we need at our castle's feet

Here at the beach
within reach of the sea.

If we can make a good moat,
we might keep it afloat."

At least that's what
my grandpa told me.

A green-eyed, blinking cat, all white and black,
Sits in the driveway watching Poppa and me.
My bike's on its back 'cause one tire's gone flat,
And Poppa is mending my puncture for free.

He says, "Watch me now, and I'll show you how
My poppa showed me what to do.
See, I've marked the right spot, now check if
we've got
Enough of the right patches and glue."

Soon I pass him the pump and before long,
I jump
Back on my bike, and the cat's got a fright
'Cause I'm riding fast on the tire Poppa fixed
And it's as good as if it were new!

The sky's a bit hazy, and the dog's going crazy.
He's running in circles 'round Andre and me.
The wind is quite strong, and the kite tail is long,
But I'm sure it's the length it should be.

I'm teaching my brother this kite-flying thing,
He's holding it high while I run the string.
I've run it right out when I hear him shout.
The kite's soaring high in the wind-whipped sky
And my brother is laughing and dancing
with glee.

Make Connections

How has the speaker in the poem shown what
she values about the things she has done with
her family? ESSENTIAL QUESTION

Compare the events that make special memories
in *Tell Me the Old, Old Stories* and in *Family Ties*.
TEXT TO TEXT

Focus on Literary Elements

Alliteration Alliteration is the repetition of the same beginning consonant sound in two or more words close together. Poets often use alliteration to make the words or lines in a poem flow in a musical way.

Read and Find In *Family Ties*, the poet uses alliteration several times. In the last stanza, "He's holding it high" and "wind-whipped" are two examples. The alliteration helps connect the words. Look for more instances of alliteration in the poem.

Your Turn

Write a short list poem using alliteration. First, list two or three people you know. Next, write one or two lines that describe each person or what you do together. Use words that start with the same sound as each person's name. Read the lines aloud and make changes to help the words express what you mean clearly.

Share your poem with a friend. Have your words expressed some things that are important to you?